ANGER MANAGEMENT

Participant Workbook

A Court-Approved Guide to Healing Unresolved G.R.I.E.F. and
Managing Anger for Personal and Legal Success

Dr. Arleen A. Fuller, Ph.D.

 Table of Contents

INTRODUCTION

Welcome to anger management. Your counselor/facilitator is here to help you decrease episodes of anger and aggressive behavior. If you want to get the most out of this group, you need to be honest with yourself and deal with the underlying issues that led you to this group.

This group is not designed to attack you. It is designed to help you. Our goal is to deliver information that will help you examine your life and evaluate your choices so you may be a happier, healthier, human being.

Class objectives

- ✓ To help you manage and control your response to anger.
- ✓ Evaluate perception, values, thought management, and conditioning.
- ✓ Help reduce the number of negative outbursts.
- ✓ Prevent emotional hijacking.
- ✓ Promote self-awareness, preventative strategies, social skills, and personal development.

WHAT IS ANGER?

Anger is a powerful emotion that can take over a person's ability to think rationally. Anger causes the brain to process incoming data as a threat and this triggers the brain to implement the fight or flight response.

Anger can be described as a negative internal feeling state that can range from mild irritation to rage and can be expressed verbally or non-verbally. It's an automatic reaction to any real or imagined insult, frustration, or injustice.

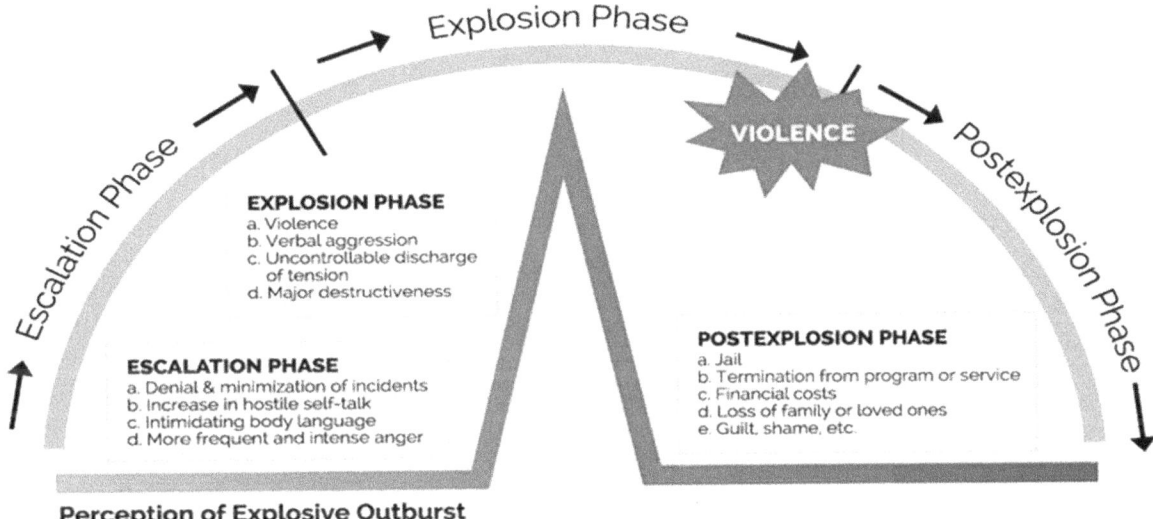

Escalation Phase

Explosion Phase

VIOLENCE

Postexplosion Phase

EXPLOSION PHASE
a. Violence
b. Verbal aggression
c. Uncontrollable discharge of tension
d. Major destructiveness

ESCALATION PHASE
a. Denial & minimization of incidents
b. Increase in hostile self-talk
c. Intimidating body language
d. More frequent and intense anger

POSTEXPLOSION PHASE
a. Jail
b. Termination from program or service
c. Financial costs
d. Loss of family or loved ones
e. Guilt, shame, etc.

Perception of Explosive Outburst

Please note that anger is an emotion that we are born with. Anger is one of the many emotions that we experience as a human being. We are born with happiness, sadness, anger, etc. Many believe that anger is bad. This is not true. Anger is an emotion that informs us that something is wrong. Anger management teaches us that we have two choices after we get angry. We have a good choice and a bad choice. Anger management teaches us to make good choices.

Negative Aspects of Anger

- ✓ False perceptions of reality can be created
- ✓ Limited views or distorted views can be developed
- ✓ Clouded thinking
- ✓ Lowers IQ
- ✓ It can make one mentally or emotionally/spiritually weak
- ✓ Anger can hurt others

Some Physical Symptoms of Anger Related Problems

- ✓ Clenching your jaws or grinding your teeth
- ✓ Headaches
- ✓ Stomach aches

- ✓ Increased and rapid heart rate
- ✓ Sweating, especially your palms
- ✓ Feeling hot in the neck/face
- ✓ Shaking or trembling
- ✓ Dizziness

Anger is a problem when it…

- ✓ Disturbs personal and professional relationships
- ✓ When it is normalized
- ✓ Too intense
- ✓ Leads to aggression
- ✓ Last too long
- ✓ Hurts others

Positive aspects of anger

- ✓ Anger can be used for good.
- ✓ Anger can be used as motivational tool.
- ✓ Anger can promote change.
- ✓ Anger can lead to assertive behavior.
- ✓ Anger can help one defend themselves from mistreatment or abuse.
- ✓ Anger is a form of self-awareness that informs us that something is wrong.

Seeds of Anger

Below is a list of reasons why some people are angry.

Place a checkmark next to any that apply to you.

_____ Family History

_____ Substance Abuse

_____ Poor Financial Management

_____ Societal Influences

_____ Physical Abuse

_____ Jealousy and Envy

_____ Resentment

_____ Lack of Professional Development

_____ Lack of Commitment (quits when times get hard)

_____ Poor Decision Making

_____ Excessive Spending

_____ Poor Values

_____ Lack of Comfort

_____ Hunger

_____ Heat

_____ Poor Mental and Physical Health

_____ Regret

_____ Failure

_____ Working or Living in a Hostile Environment

_____ Poor Self-Talk

_____ Lying to Oneself

_____ Listening to the Wrong People

_____ Limited thinking

_____ Failure to live authentically

_____ Other(s): _____

UNDERLYING FEELINGS ASSOCIATED WITH ANGER

Source: Seltzer, L. F. (2008). What your anger may be hiding. Retrieved from

https://www.psychologytoday.com/blog/evolution-the-self/200807/what-your-anger-may-be-hiding

Anger has been described as a secondary emotion, meaning that it results from another, primary emotion which occurred first. Put simply, this means that the feeling of anger may be masking an underlying feeling such as fear, hurt, or shame. When we acknowledge that we are scared or hurt, we may feel vulnerable or weak. Anger provides a way for us to feel more powerful. The problem with that, however, is that anger can lead to aggression and other problematic behaviors.

Let's look at a few scenarios that show how anger can be masking underlying emotions:

Daniel was driving down the highway when another car suddenly merged in front of him and cut him off. Daniel tensed up and his heart began to beat faster. In response to this event, he slammed on his horn and shouted expletives at the driver who cut him off.

What emotions might Daniel have been experiencing?

_____

_____

_____

_____

Juan recently got into an argument with his girlfriend after finding out that she had been texting a male coworker after hours. He angrily accused her of cheating on him, and called her derogatory names.

What emotions might Juan have been experiencing?

_____

_____

_____

_____

_____

Susan was with a group of friends when she made a joke that others found offensive. Her friends expressed their discomfort with the joke, and Susan responded by accusing them of being too sensitive. She began yelling at them.

What emotions might Susan have been feeling?

_____

_____

_____

_____

_____

The above scenarios show how anger may be used to express other underlying emotions. Anger can help us feel more powerful and in control when we are vulnerable to feeling weak and powerless.

Can you think of a time in your own life when your anger masked other feelings?

_____

_____

_____

_____

_____

When you are hurt, how do you typically express it?

_____

_____

_____

_____

When you are scared, how do you typically express it?

_____

_____

_____

_____

When you feel embarrassed or ashamed, how do you express it?

_____

_____

_____

_____

_____

Do you feel comfortable expressing anger? Why or why not?

_____

_____

_____

_____

_____

ANGER AND CULTURE

Source: Laurent, S. (2015). Are men angrier than women? Retrieved from
https://www.psychologytoday.com/blog/chill-pill/201505/are-men-angrier-women

The way that we express and deal with anger and other emotions is influenced by cultural factors, such as gender. For example, men are often taught that it is not acceptable to cry or show vulnerability, while women are considered to be unladylike if they express anger. Research shows that men are more likely than women to use physical force when they feel angry. It is important to understand how your culture impacts your emotions.

In your opinion, what emotions are acceptable for men to express? Which are unacceptable?

_____

_____

_____

_____

_____

What emotions are acceptable for women to express? Which are unacceptable?

_____

_____

_____

_____

_____

How do people in your culture express anger?

_____

_____

_____

_____

_____

What beliefs do you have about emotions based on cultural factors?

_____

_____

_____

_____

_____

ANGER MANAGEMENT STRATEGIES

It is not realistic to expect that you will never feel angry. Instead, focus on ways that you can manage your anger in a healthy way, rather than acting out in violent or aggressive ways. Some anger management skills are preventative, meaning that they can reduce your overall anger and increase your emotional stability. Some, on the other hand, are designed to be used in the moment, when you are feeling angry or otherwise triggered. Here are some healthy coping skills for managing anger:

- Exercise
- Remove yourself from the event that is triggering you
- Practice deep breathing and progressive muscle relaxation exercises
- Change your perception of the situation
- Listen to music
- Watch something that makes you laugh in order to change your mood
- Work on personal/professional goals
- Try to see the "big picture" and think rationally
- Understand how prescription drugs affect your body
- Don't engage in conversations that you feel uncomfortable about (ex: politics or religion)
- Do something that makes you feel good
- Get adequate food and rest
- Be financially responsible
- Know your triggers so that you can be prepared for them or avoid them when necessary
- Let go of the past
- Stop drug or alcohol use
- Plan ahead of time
- Engage in self-care (massages, vacation, grooming)
- Practice being assertive

THE A-B-C-D MODEL FOR ANGER MANAGEMENT

Source: Pratt, K. (2014). Psychology tools: A-B-C-D model for anger management. Retrieved from https://healthypsych.com/psychology-tools-a-b-c-d-model-for-anger-management/

The A-B-C-D model is a technique developed by Albert Ellis that is used frequently in Cognitive Behavioral Therapy (CBT). This technique involves identifying the event that triggered anger and the beliefs that contribute to it, and then disputing those irrational beliefs. Using the A-B-C-D model can help you to gain a more rational perspective on your anger.

Identify irrational beliefs and dispute them with more rational or realistic perspectives.

A = Activating Situation (Trigger)

Example: Somebody cuts you off in traffic while you are driving to work.

B = Belief System

What you tell yourself about the event (self-talk). Your beliefs and expectations of others.

Example: This person is such a jerk! He is a terrible driver!

C = Consequence

How you feel about the event based on your self-talk. It is important to note that the consequences are not based on the event itself, but on your beliefs about it! Example: You yell out the window, honk your horn, and shout expletives at the other driver.

D = Dispute:

Examine your beliefs and expectations. Are they unrealistic or irrational? Are there alternative beliefs that could explain the event?

Example: Maybe the other driver was driving recklessly because he had an emergency, or perhaps he was distracted because something tragic happened to him earlier in the day.

These new beliefs can help you to consider other perspectives so that you can remain calmer.

Now try applying to A-B-C-D model to a recent event from your own life. Think about a recent time when you felt angry or upset:

What was the Activating Event?

_____

_____

_____

_____

_____

What were your Beliefs about the situation? What did you tell yourself about it?

_____

_____

_____

_____

_____

What were the Consequences of those beliefs? What actions did you take?

_____

_____

_____

_____

_____

What alternative beliefs may have explained (or Disputed) the situation? What could you have told yourself in order to remain calmer?

_____

_____

_____

_____

_____

MASTER YOUR EMOTIONS

If you can control your emotions, you can control your life. Some describe this as emotional intelligence. Imagine if you were always in the mood to workout, study, and perform your duties at a high level. Using this power can improve your life.

So how do we manipulate our emotions? We find out what drives us. We can use the power of music, environment, movies or nostalgia to change our mood. Have you ever listened to some music that made you want to get active? Have you ever watched a movie or television show that made you want to workout?

When you watch a movie you are not consciously aware of how the background music is changing your mood. You are just watching the movie and trying to enjoy the experience. But the makers of the film are trying to get you emotionally involved by playing scary music in the background to enhance your feeling of fear. Or they may play sad music in the background during a traumatic scene to make you feel sadness. During a car chase or action scene, they play upbeat music to get you excited. During this whole experience your focus is not on the background music, it is on the film. You have been unconsciously influenced by music and you didn't even notice it.

Let me be clear; I am not telling you to go watch movies all day. I am giving you an example of how music and film can influence your mood.

You can use the same tricks that movies and commercials use to influence your buying decisions and behavior. This requires self-awareness. What makes you focused? Figure it out and do it before you need to study. What makes you calm? Figure it out and do it when you need to relax. Do things that will influence you to be the person you desire to be at the right place and the right time. Do what works for you. Everyone is different.

There are some people like myself that watch the training montages from movies or videos online to get in the mood to workout. Do whatever works for you.

Know yourself and manipulate your mind to do what you want it to do. You are the puppet master. You hold the controls to motivate yourself. Use this formula if you need to get motivated.

High Purpose + High Emotion =Motivation

You need to have a strong reason to change if you are going to change. I call that your "why" or "purpose." We can also change the equation to look like this.

High Value + High Emotion= Motivation

You need to see the value in changing if you are going to change. And the value needs to be high. You have to see the value in it. Combine this with a strong emotion or desire to change, you will then develop the motivation you need.

MOOD MANAGEMENT STRATEGIES

Music – Listen to enjoyable music. Listening to your favorite songs can improve your mood. Music is a powerful tool that has been used in movies to enhance emotions of fear, joy, sadness, excitement, etc. Imagine watching a scary movie without background music or sound effects. It wouldn't be as scary. You can use music to change your mood.

Nostalgia – Reminisce about happy times in your past. Review old pictures, movies, or television series that you used to enjoy. Do things that you used to enjoy, that you don't do now.

Self-Care – Take care of yourself. Get a massage, pedicure, manicure, etc. Go on vacation and eat healthy food. Exercise to increase your production of endorphins. With high endorphin levels, we feel less pain and fewer negative effects of stress. Endorphins have been suggested as modulators of the so-called "runner's high" that athletes achieve with prolonged exercise.

Self-Talk – Monitor or be mindful of what you say to yourself. Try to be positive and say things to yourself that uplift you instead of bring you down. Negative self-talk is not healthy and can destroy your life.

Journaling – Write down what is on your mind. By journaling, you can evaluate your life and express yourself honestly. Act out your emotions on paper. Later, you can review your entries and decide if you were being rational or being irrational.

You can review your journal to remind yourself of previous accomplishments, lessons, and how you have overcome obstacles. Journaling is a great tool for personal growth.

Change Environment – Some people live, work, or go to school in negative environments. You would be surprised how exposure to different people, places, or things can improve your life. If you are in a negative environment, consider changing it to a positive one. Your odds of living a happy life increase when you are in a positive environment.

Counseling – Sometimes people become overwhelmed and are unable to cope with life's stressors. If this is the case for you, consider seeing a counselor. A professional counselor can assist you with challenging issues in your life.

Receiving guidance from a neutral party who has no emotional attachment to the situation may bring clarity.

Stress Prevention Strategies – Do things ahead of time in order to prevent future stressful events from occurring. We want you to anticipate needs. Examples include: budgeting, planning ahead, paying bills on time, leaving early from work to avoid traffic, getting things done before you are asked, telling people "no," etc.

Things that can influence your mood

Caffeine

Food

Pictures

Scents

Hunger

Thirst

Clothes

Heat

Noise

Music

Silence

Looking

Good

Looking

Bad

Brightness

Dimness

Humor

People Rest

Events

Colors

Exercise

Finances

Medication

Grooming

Cleanliness

Body

Image

Sex

Health Love

Stress/Pressure

Animals

Children

Accomplishment

Someone else's vibes

Nostalgia

Massage

Color

Puzzles

Adversity

Opportunity

Injustice

Prejudice

Alcohol

Drugs

Gambling

Shopping

Winning

Losing

RELAXATION SKILLS

Sources: Davis, M, Eshelman, E. R., & McKay, M. (2008). The relaxation & stress reduction workbook, 6th edition. Oakland, CA: New Harbinger Publications, Inc.

Ray, L. (2013). Box breathing technique. Retrieved from http://www.livestrong.com/article/74944-box-breathing-technique/

When you notice that tension is building, it can be helpful to use relaxation as a way to control your emotions so that you don't get overwhelmed or aggressive or otherwise behave in problematic ways. It is best to use these skills as soon as you recognize that you are starting to feel irritable, frustrated, or upset. If you wait until your feelings escalate, relaxation will be more challenging. Practicing these relaxation skills each day, even when you aren't feeling stressed or upset, can be especially beneficial because it helps to keep your stress level low, so that you are less susceptible to emotional upsets or outbursts.

Breathing

Breathing exercises have been shown to be effective for reducing anxiety, irritability, and muscle tension.

It is important to make sure that you are breathing correctly. Diaphragmatic (abdominal) breathing is ideal. To ensure that you are breathing diaphragmatically, place one hand on your stomach and one on your chest. You should feel the hand on your stomach rise with each inhalation, while the hand on your chest remains mostly still.

Practice: Place one hand on your stomach and one on your chest. Take a few deep breaths and notice which hand moves. Continue until the hand on your stomach rises with each inhalation and falls with each exhalation.

Here are a couple of breathing exercises that can be a useful way to manage stress, anger, or other emotional upsets:

1. Breathing to let go of tension: Inhale (diaphragmatically) while saying "breathe in" to yourself. Hold your breath for a moment. Exhale slowly as you tell yourself to "relax." Pause and repeat. With each inhalation, notice the parts of your body that tense up. As you exhale, feel the tension leaving your body. If you get distracted by thoughts, feelings, or sensations, simply return your focus to your breathing. Practice this exercise for 5-20 minutes.
2. Square breathing technique: Sit in a comfortable chair with your feet on the floor. Maintain a relaxed posture. Close your mouth and breathe in slowly for a count of four. Hold your breath for four seconds, before opening your mouth slightly and exhaling for four seconds. Then hold for another count of four. Repeat for up to four minutes.

Progressive Muscle Relaxation

Progressive muscle relaxation is an effective way to let go of stress and tension in your body. Like any relaxation skill, it takes practice to master. Follow these steps to try progressive muscle relaxation:

1. Get into a comfortable position in a quiet room.
2. Close your eyes and took a few deep breaths.
3. Tense the muscles in your feet and hold them in that tensed position for a count of three.
4. Relax the muscles in your feet.
5. Next, repeat steps 3 and 4 with your calves.
6. Continue tensing and relaxing each part of your body, up to your head.

What other relaxation skills can you identify?

_____

_____

_____

_____

_____

TOLERATING DISTRESS

Source: McKay, M., Wood, J. C., & Brantley, J. (2007). The Dialectical behavior therapy skills workbook. Oakland, CA: New Harbinger Publications.

We all experience times of emotional overwhelm and distress, despite our best efforts to manage our moods. Pain, whether physical or emotional, is an unavoidable part of life. Fortunately, we do not have to resort to aggression or violence when we feel distressed. Instead, we can learn to tolerate our distress so that we can more effectively deal with our problems and manage our emotions. Here are some skills for coping with feelings of distress and pain:

- Distraction—Although it is usually not beneficial to avoid an issue forever, it can be smart to temporarily distract from it until you feel more able to handle it. If you are feeling too overwhelmed with a situation, try distracting yourself temporarily. You can distract yourself by engaging in a pleasurable activity, doing tasks/chores, focusing on another person (for example, calling a friend and asking him/her to tell you about what is happening in their life). You can also try distracting your thoughts by counting, fantasizing, focusing on the natural world around you, or reciting a favorite prayer or saying.
- Self-soothing—Just as a crying baby wants to be soothed, we want to feel comforted and relaxed when we are in pain. To soothe yourself, try using one of your five senses. For example, take a warm bath, listen to relaxing music, visualize a relaxing scene, or snuggle up with a soft blanket.
- Replace negative thinking with positive, encouraging thoughts—When you're upset, it's easy to wallow in your misery and focus only on the pain. Instead, try using encouraging self-talk. Repeat things like, "This too shall pass" and "I'm strong enough to handle this."

Identify 3 ways that you can distract yourself when you feel overwhelmed:

_____

_____

_____

_____

_____

Identify 3 ways that you can soothe yourself:

_____

_____

_____

_____

_____

List 3 encouraging thoughts that you can say to yourself in times of distress:

_____

_____

_____

_____

_____

MINDFULNESS

Source: McKay, M., Wood, J. C., & Brantley, J. (2007). The Dialectical behavior therapy skills workbook. Oakland, CA: New Harbinger Publications.

To be mindful is to be aware of your emotions without judging them. It means that you are not telling yourself that you should or shouldn't feel a certain way, but are rather allowing your emotions to exist. Being mindful can help to decrease the intensity of your emotions, so that you are less likely to act in aggressive or otherwise problematic ways.

Follow these steps to increase your ability to be mindful:

1. Focus on your breath. Breathe slowly and evenly and bring your attention to your breath.
2. Focus on the emotion that you are feeling.
3. Notice the physical sensations connected to the emotion. Where do you feel it in your body? Perhaps your stomach hurts, or your shoulders feel tight.
4. Name the emotion.
5. Notice any judgments that may be present and simply let them go. Picture each judgment as a leaf floating down a stream, and simply let it pass. Repeat this step as needed.
6. Remind yourself that your feelings are valid.
7. Take some deep breaths.

Although mindfulness sounds simple in concept, it takes practice. Whenever you get distracted, simply return your focus to your breath. With time and effort, you will start to notice that you are more aware of your emotions, which will allow you to have more control over them.

EMOTIONAL INTELLIGENCE

Emotional intelligence (EI) is the ability to perceive, control and evaluate emotions in yourself and others. EI is also ability to understand verbal and nonverbal communication that is presented in any given situation. You can use perception, self-awareness, and mood management strategies to make the right decisions, at the right place, at the right times, to excel in life. The first step is to learn how to manage your mood. Please provide solutions to the situations listed below.

When you are annoyed, you will do this to improve your mood:

_____

When you are angry, you will do this to improve your mood:

_____

When you are depressed, you will do this to improve your mood:

_____

When you feel disrespected, you will do this to improve your mood:

_____

When you don't feel like exercising, you will do this to put you in the mood:

_____

When you feel like using alcohol or drugs, you will do this to change your mood:

_____

When you don't feel like controlling your mouth, you will do this to change your mood:

_____

When you are bored, you will do this to keep your mind occupied:

When you don't feel like studying, you will do this to change your mood:

_____

When you don't feel like going to work, you will do this to change your mood:

_____

When you are sleepy and need to wake up, you will do this:

_____

When you are lonely, you will do this:

_____

When you feel heartbroken, you will do this to improve your mood:

_____

When you are running late, you will do this to calm down:

_____

Add your own personal scenarios below that may occur in your life. After you write them, write down how you are going to deal with them in a healthy manner.

_____

Components of Emotional Intelligence

Source: Cherry, K. (2016). Five components of emotional intelligence. Retrieved from https://www.verywell.com/components-of-emotional-intelligence-2795438

Emotional intelligence consists of five distinct skills and abilities:

1. Self-awareness: This refers to the ability to understand our own emotions, and how our behaviors affect other people.
2. Self-regulation: Self-regulation involves the ability to manage our emotions effectively, so that we can express them appropriately. The ability to self-regulate prevents us from acting aggressively or in other problematic ways.

3. Social skills: Social skills include active listening, communication skills, and leadership abilities. Social skills allow us to form and maintain good relationships with others.
4. Empathy: This is the ability to understand how another person might be feeling.
5. Motivation: Motivation helps us to achieve our goals. Intrinsic (or internal) motivation is typically more effective than external motivation. Having intrinsic motivation means that we are driven by our own inner goals and values, rather than being motivated by external factors such as money, reward, or praise.

Which of these areas are you strongest in?

_____

_____

_____

_____

_____

Which area needs the most improvement?

_____

_____

_____

_____

_____

List 3 specific things you can do to improve your emotional intelligence.

_____

_____

_____

_____

PERCEPTION

How we view or see things can influence our thought process and behavior. Inaccurate perceptions of situations can lead to negative thinking, negative behavior, and negative consequences. There is power in perception. Have you ever viewed something as hard to achieve and then when you tried it, it was easy? Or have you ever viewed something as easy and it was actually hard? Or have you ever had the wrong perception of someone or something? We have to be mindful of our perceptions. Everything is not always what it seems to be and we need to make sure that we are looking through the right lens.

What is your perception of being in anger management? Please be honest.

_____

_____

_____

_____

_____

How did you come to this conclusion? Is it based on your personal experience or what others have told you?

_____

_____

_____

_____

_____

Do you have the right perception? Are you looking through the right lens?

_____

_____

_____

_____

_____

_____

Many people say that "seeing is believing." Is this true or false? Please explain.

_____

_____

_____

_____

_____

_____

_____

_____

_____

The statement "seeing is believing" is based on perception. There are those that will never manage their anger because they don't see themselves having a problem. They will rationalize or defend their behavior because they perceive it as acceptable. They may even believe or perceive that other people are the ones that have the real problem.

What perception do you have of yourself? What do you believe about yourself? Please be honest.

_____

_____

_____

_____

_____

Sometimes having the wrong perception can trigger people lose control of their emotions. Has this ever happened to you? If so, what can you do to make sure this doesn't happen again?

_____

_____

_____

_____

_____

What is the difference between being rational and irrational?

_____

_____

_____

_____

_____

What can you do to make sure you make rational choices?

_____

_____

_____

_____

_____

Many people say "I don't care what other people think." But many are lying to themselves. What strategies can you use to keep a positive mindset if someone perceives you the wrong way?

_____

_____

_____

_____

_____

If you were failed to manage your anger on a regular basis what would be the possible consequences?

_____

_____

_____

_____

_____

_____

ERRORS IN PERCEPTION

Nobody perceives things exactly as they are; we all make errors in perception. These errors are especially likely to occur when we are overwhelmed by emotion, because it can be difficult to remain rational in those times. Here are some types of common perception errors, or cognitive distortions.

- Overgeneralizing—making a general conclusion from a single piece of evidence. Ex: Assuming that you are stupid because you got a low score on one test
- Jumping to conclusions—assuming that you know what will happen in the future. Ex: assuming that you will get fired from your job because you were late one time
- Mind reading—assuming that you know what another person is thinking/feeling
- Black and white thinking—extreme thinking in which there is no middle ground. Example: seeing an individual as either perfect or horrible, rather than acknowledging that we all have both good and bad qualities
- Emotional reasoning—believing that just because you feel a certain way, something is true. Ex: Believing that you are a failure just because you are feeling bad about yourself at a given moment.
- Catastrophizing—making things seem worse than they really are. Ex: assuming that your partner is going to leave you because you had one argument
- Personalization—taking blame or responsibility for things that are not actually your fault. Ex: a child may believe that his parents would not have gotten divorced if he had behaved better
- Shoulds—telling yourself that you "should" be a certain way, or expecting others to be the way that you want them to be. Ex: Believing that others "should" always behave the way you want, despite their own wishes and needs
- Filtering—Only acknowledging evidence that confirms a negative conclusion. Ex: paying attention only to the bad things that one has done, while discounting any successes
- Labeling—using negative labels to describe yourself or others. Ex: calling somebody an "idiot" or other derogatory name because he cuts in front of you in line

Which of these cognitive distortions do you make most often?

_____

_____

_____

_____

How might these errors in perception contribute to anger and aggression?

_____

_____

_____

_____

_____

ANGER COPING THOUGHTS

Source: Davis, M, Eshelman, E. R., & McKay, M. (2008). The relaxation & stress reduction workbook, 6th edition. Oakland, CA: New Harbinger Publications, Inc.

When your perception is distorted, you are not thinking clearly. If you are blaming others, catastrophizing, jumping to conclusions, or overgeneralizing, you are likely to feel angrier than the situation warrants. Using coping statements can help you to decrease your anger and respond appropriately to the situation.

Here are some examples of coping thoughts that you can use when you begin to feel angry:

- Blaming makes me feel helpless. What can I do to change the situation?
- I'm upset but the other person is doing his/her best.
- This too shall pass.
- I can handle this.
- This is annoying, but I probably won't even remember it in a few days.
- How bad is this situation really?
- The other person does not intend to upset me.
- Getting angry won't help.
- Stay calm.
- I have the ability to remain relaxed.
- I can't change the other person.
- I'm not going to let the other person get to me.
- No matter what, I know that I am a good person.
- It's not the end of the world.

What other thoughts might help you keep your anger in check?

_____

_____

_____

_____

_____

_____

SELF-ACTUALIZATION

Create a plan and write down the things that you can do now to become your ideal self.

_____

_____

_____

_____

_____

_____

_____

_____

_____

_____

_____

_____

_____

_____

_____

_____

_____

_____

_____

_____

_____

_____

PREVENTION PLAN

Prevention Plans are created to assist in monitoring behavior patterns and gives you the ability to make adjustments. This tool will assist you in examining your behavior and creating positive alternative choices when you are triggered to do something negative due to being angry. Please write down your triggers and your usual response to them. After that is complete, write down the same triggers and a positive alternative response for each trigger.

Trigger	Negative Response
Example: Failure	Response: Go get drunk

Trigger	Positive Response
Example: Failure	Response: I'm going to view this as a learning process and I understand that many people fail. Now is not the time to be irrational and find an excuse to drink. I will take a break and do something that improves my mood. When I am ready, I will try again.

AVOIDING TRIGGERS

You may have heard some people that are in recovery say "be smart, not strong." This implies that we can avoid returning to negative behavior patterns by using better judgment. If we are smart, we do not have to be strong. Certain people, places, or things can trigger negative behavior patterns or relapse. By placing yourself in these situations, it will require you to be strong. Many of us think we are strong, but we are really not. Choose to be smart and avoid your triggers.

In the boxes below, please list the people, places, and things that you need to avoid.

People	Places	Things

What discussion topics do you need to avoid?

_____

_____

_____

_____

_____

_____

_____

_____

_____

DENIAL

Denial is something that we must address in anger management. There are those in group that will give a million excuses to why they do the things that they do. They will rationalize their behavior and defend choices by bringing up statistics, laws in other countries, scientific studies, etc. Most of them know what they are saying is full of you-know-what. They are not fooling the counselor or the people around them. They are just fooling themselves.

What are you in denial about? Denial can be a seed of anger. Here is a list of things that some people are in denial about:

Relationships   Career Choice

Eating Habits   Fame

Getting Older   Spending Habits

Exercising   Illness

Family History   Work Ethic

School Work   Their Children

Substance Use   Appearance

Can you add to this list? What are people in denial about?

_____

_____

_____

_____

_____

Why do you think some people live in denial?

_____

_____

_____

_____

_____

Is this healthy?

Yes or No

What are you in denial about? Are you going to stay in denial or change?

_____

_____

_____

_____

_____

Does denial truly help you? Please explain.

_____

_____

_____

_____

_____

What would you like to change? Put a check next to all that apply to you.

_____ Substance Use	_____ Commitment
_____ Excessive Spending	_____ Values
_____ Financial Management	_____ Decision Making
_____ Spouse	_____ Education Level
_____ Peer Group	_____ Temperament
_____ Physical Health	_____ Thought Process
_____ Abusive Behavior	_____ Discipline
_____ Career	_____ Criminal Behavior
_____ Jealousy and Envy	_____ Mental Health
_____ Work Environment	_____ Negative Thinking
_____ Resentment	
_____ Self-Talk	

STAGES OF CHANGE

Stage 1: Pre-contemplation (Not Ready)

Individuals do not see their behavior as a problem in this stage. Those in the

Pre-contemplation stage do not intend to take action in the foreseeable future, even if they have experienced negative consequences for their actions.

Stage 2: Contemplation (Getting Ready)

Contemplation is the stage in which people are aware of the pros and cons of changing their behavior. Instead of defending their behavior, they evaluate, and consider the idea of changing. Continuously weighing the costs and benefits of changing can produce chronic contemplation or procrastination.

Stage 3: Preparation

Preparation is the stage to take action and do specific things that promote change. These individuals have a plan of action, such as going to therapy, talking to their physician, buying a self-help book, scheduling, creating a budget, etc.

Stage 4: Action

Action is the stage in which people have made specific, overt modifications in their lifestyles. Observers from the outside, like friends, relatives, and co-workers will notice that change is occurring. Specific actions are taken to promote lifestyle changes.

Stage 5: Maintenance

Maintenance is the stage in which people have made positive lifestyle choices and have been successful at avoiding relapse. While in the Maintenance stage, people are less tempted to relapse and grow increasingly more confident that they can continue their changes.

What stage of change are you in for the selection that applied to you?

_____ Substance Use   _____ Abusive Behavior

_____ Negative Thinking   _____ Physical Health

_____ Financial Management   _____ Jealousy and Envy

_____ Excessive Spending   _____ Career

_____ Peer Group   _____ Resentment

_____ Spouse   _____ Work Environment

_____ Commitment   _____ Education Level

_____ Self-Talk   _____ Discipline

_____ Decision Making   _____ Thought Process

_____ Values   _____ Mental Health

_____ Temperament   _____ Criminal Behavior

How can you improve your weak areas?

_____

_____

_____

_____

_____

MOTIVATION TO CHANGE

Motivation to change usually occurs when there is a perceived purpose or benefit to change. Many people minimize their behavior, make multiple excuses, or say "Why should I change?" In the back of their minds, they know that change requires work and they have become comfortable with their habits.

Change requires discipline and work. Everyone likes a job with benefits. But to get the benefits, you have to do the work. In this section, we want you to weigh the long-term pros and cons of changing your behavior. We want you to find your purpose.

Pros	Cons

Pros	Cons

COMMUNICATION SKILLS

Source: Allen, R. (2012), SMART recovery family and friends handbook. Alcohol & Drug Abuse Self-Help Network, Inc.

In order to manage your anger, you need to know how to communicate with others in healthy ways. Yelling or acting aggressively is likely to make a situation more stressful, and potentially dangerous. However, if you are able to communicate effectively, you may be able to reduce the likelihood that your anger will get out of control.

Effective communication involves expressing empathy and understanding, and making the other person feel heard and understood. Here are some basic communication skills that can improve your ability to be effective when dealing with other people:

1. Ask open ended questions—Asking open-ended questions (that cannot be answered with a simple yes or no) allows the other person the opportunity to express their thoughts and feelings. It is a great way to get more information about a situation and to express that you want to understand the other person's perspective.
2. Reflective listening—Reflective listening involves fully listening to the other person is saying, and then reflecting back what you heard without disagreeing or arguing. Reflective listening is a way to convey empathy, so that the other person feels understood. It has the ability to build a greater sense of trust between two people.
3. Offer validation—We all want to feel heard and understood, and offering validation is one way to facilitate that. When you offer validation, you are essentially letting the other person know that you understand and appreciate how they are feeling. This is a great way to reduce defensiveness and build trust.

Practice Exercises:

Rephrase the following closed questions as open-ended questions:

1. Did you have a good day?

_____

_____

_____

2. Are you upset?

_____

3. Do you enjoy sports?

_____

_____

_____

_____

_____

Write a reflective listening statement that demonstrates that you understand what the speaker said:

1. Speaker: "I'm so mad right now. I can't believe that you came home late!"

_____

_____

_____

2. Speaker: "I feel really bad that I showed up late to work today. I hope that my boss doesn't fire me."

_____

_____

_____

To validate somebody's feelings, it can be helpful to start with the phrase "I understand that you feel..." Write a validation statement for each of the following scenarios:

1. You come across a motorist who is stranded on the side of a busy freeway during a rain storm. She seems very flustered as she tries to figure out how to fix a flat tire on her car.

I understand that you feel _____

_____

2. You respond to a call about possible domestic violence. When you arrive at the home, you find a woman who is very reluctant to open the door.

I understand that you feel_____

_____

3. You arrive at the scene of a domestic dispute. The woman begins yelling at you, saying that you took way to long to arrive at the scene.

I understand that you feel _____

_____

In order to express empathy and communicative effectively, it's important to pay attention to not just the words you say, but also to how you are communicating. You send a message through nonverbal cues, such as your posture, tone of voice, and facial expression.

How can you express empathy through your facial expressions?

_____

_____

_____

What posture should you maintain to show that you want to help, and are not a threat?

_____

_____

_____

How can you convey empathy through your tone of voice?

_____

_____

_____

What nonverbal cues should you avoid?

_____

_____

_____

_____

_____

_____

_____

_____

ASSERTIVENESS

Assertiveness involves standing up for your rights and expressing feelings, thoughts, and beliefs in direct, honest, and appropriate ways that do not disrespect or violate the rights of others.

What is assertiveness?

- ✓ Stating your ideas confidently, directly and with clarity.
- ✓ Confronting difficult issues in without insulting or putting down others.
- ✓ Expressing your concerns, wants or needs.

Benefits from being assertive

- ✓ Protects one from being abused or taken advantage of
- ✓ Promotes dialogue and examination of issues
- ✓ Builds self-esteem
- ✓ Clarifies position or stance
- ✓ Increases honesty, requests, refusals
- ✓ Promotes negotiation
- ✓ Decreases regret

What assertiveness is NOT

- ✓ Manipulation
- ✓ Hostility or Aggressiveness
- ✓ Passive Aggressiveness

How to Communicate Assertively

"I" statements: Start by stating how you feel, rather than blaming the other person for the situation. Ex: I feel hurt when…

Provide specific examples rather than generalizations: Rather than stating that somebody "always" or "never" does something, try to provide specific examples of problematic behavior so that the other person has a clear idea of what bothered you. Saying, "I felt hurt when you didn't answer my call" is more effective than saying "you never answer my calls!".

Take responsibility for your own role: In any relationship, both people contribute to issues and problems. If you are willing to take responsibility for your own role, the other person is usually more willing to acknowledge theirs

Don't yell: Maintain a calm, composed voice. If you find yourself getting upset or yelling, take a few deep breaths to regain your composure. If necessary, take a brief time out and resume the conversation at a time when you feel calmer.

Acknowledge the positives: Nobody behaves badly all the time. Acknowledging the other person's good intentions or positive actions can set the tone for a more positive conversation. Let them know what you appreciate about them.

Make a request: When expressing a desire for somebody to change their behavior, make a clear and simple request. Ex: I would appreciate it if you would not talk to me while I'm on the phone with another person.

Express gratitude/appreciation: Let the other person know that you appreciate their willingness to listen and make changes in their own behavior.

Listen—Being assertive means that you are considering the needs of others as well as your own needs. Make sure to really listen to the other person rather than just focusing on saying your piece.

Practice Exercise:

Think about an issue that is bothering you in a relationship, or a change that you would like somebody to make. How might you address the issue assertively?

- ✓ Start by creating an I statement: I feel _____ when (describe the problem in specific terms here)_____
  _____
  _____
  _____

- ✓ Then, make a clear, specific request: I would appreciate it if_____
  _____
  _____

- ✓ Express your appreciation/gratitude: Thank you for _____
  _____
  _____

- ✓ Is there anything else you would add to your statement? _____
  _____
  _____

What are the benefits of being assertive?

_____

_____

_____

_____

_____

How will you deal with someone who is trying to intimidate or control you?

_____

_____

_____

_____

_____

Are you willing to defend your beliefs? Why or why not?

_____

_____

_____

_____

_____

What is the difference between being assertive and being aggressive?

_____

_____

_____

_____

_____

Is sticking up for other people important? Why or why not?

_____

_____

_____

_____

_____

_____

_____

_____

Blocks To Being Assertive

Source: McKay, M., Wood, J. C., & Brantley, J. (2007). The Dialectical behavior therapy skills workbook. Oakland, CA: New Harbinger Publications.

Sometimes old habits can get in the way of effective communication. If you witnessed your family members being aggressive and blaming others for problems, then you may have learned to use those methods of communication as well.

Communication techniques that involve using fear, shame, blame, or other types of psychological pressure are not healthy. In order to stop using such techniques, you first need to be able to recognize them.

Here are some examples of unhealthy, aggressive interactions:

- Discounting: Making the other person feel that his/her feelings are unimportant and invalid. Example: "Who cares what you think?"
- Withdrawing: Sending the message that you are going to leave/abandon the other person. Example: "It's my way or the highway."
- Threatening: Threatening to cause harm or to make the other person miserable if he/she doesn't do what you want.
- Blaming: Blaming the problem entirely on the other person, rather than acknowledging your own role in it.
- Belittling: Making the other person feel silly or wrong for having a particular need. Example: "You're too stupid to understand the situation."
- Guilt-tripping: Making the other person feel guilty for having a need. Example: "I try to do so much for you, but it's never enough."
- Derailing: Moving attention away from the other person's wants/needs. Example: "I don't care how you're feeling, because now I'm upset."
- Taking away: Withholding some type of reward or pleasure as punishment.

Which of these unhealthy styles of communication have you used?

_____

_____

_____

_____

_____

HANDLING CONFLICTS

Source: Segal, J., & Smith, M. (2016). Conflict resolution skills. Retrieved from

https://www.helpguide.org/articles/relationships/conflict-resolution-skills.htm

Conflict is unavoidable, but it does not have to lead to aggression/violence. Conflict resolution skills can help you to deal with conflicts in a more effective and healthy way.

Healthy responses to conflict:

- The ability to recognize the point of view of the other person
- Calm, respectful reactions
- A willingness to seek compromise and avoid punishing
- The ability to forgive and move forward
- A willingness to address conflict head on, with a focus on conflict resolution rather than being "right"

Basics of conflict resolution:

1. Remain calm—Although conflict can be stressful, it will be more easily resolved if you can remain calm and collected. Doing so will allow you to think more rationally, and to set a calmer tone for all parties involved in the conflict. To help yourself remain calm, try taking a few deep breaths or use the techniques for tolerating distress that you identified earlier in the workbook.
2. Be emotionally aware—Recognizing your own emotions, as well as the emotions of other people, will help you to understand why the conflict is occurring and why each party is responding as they are. Pay attention to how you are feeling in the moment, and try to understand how the other person is feeling as well.
3. Pay attention to nonverbal communication—Your posture, facial expressions, and tone of voice can convey just as much information as your actual words. By appearing calm and relaxed, you can help to calm the situation down so that both parties can communicate more effectively.
4. Focus on resolving the conflict rather than being right—It's normal to want to prove that you are right, but in reality, both parties usually have some validity to their point of view. Instead of trying to prove that you are right, consider what solutions may help both parties achieve their goals.
5. Be respectful—Throughout the conflict, remain an attitude of respect for the other person and their feelings. Using derogatory language or name-calling will likely escalate the conflict rather than resolve it.

What strategies do you use when you are engaged in conflicts with different types of people?

- ✓ Those who are aggressive
- ✓ Those who are passive aggressive
- ✓ Those who avoid conflict
- ✓ Those who are silent

- ✓ Those who hold grudges
- ✓ Those who are in power positions

Aggressive

_____

_____

_____

_____

_____

Passive aggressive

_____

_____

_____

_____

_____

Avoid Conflict

_____

_____

_____

_____

_____

Silent

_____

_____

_____

_____

_____

Hold Grudges

_____

_____

_____

_____

_____

Well Connected or in Positions of Power

_____

_____

_____

_____

_____

_____

_____

_____

_____

_____

_____

_____

_____

_____

_____

_____

_____

_____

CONFLICT RESOLUTION MODEL

Conflict is unavoidable; in relationships, we are bound to have disagreements with others. However, conflict does not have to lead to fights and aggression. In fact, conflict can provide a positive opportunity for growth and change. Here are some steps for resolving conflicts in a healthy manner:

1. Identify the problem that is causing the conflict. Be specific when identifying the problem.
2. Identify the feelings associated with the conflict.
3. Identify the specific impact of the problem that is causing the conflict.
4. Decide whether to resolve the conflict or let it go. This may be best phrased by the questions, "Is the conflict important enough to bring up? If I do not try to resolve this issue, will it lead to feelings of anger and resentment?" If you decide that the conflict is important enough, then the fifth step is necessary.
5. Address and resolve the conflict. Choose an appropriate time and place to discuss the situation. Express your request simply and firmly. And remember to be willing to address your own role in the conflict!

MAKING A REQUEST

McKay, M., Wood, J. C., & Brantley, J. (2007). The Dialectical behavior therapy skills workbook. Oakland, CA: New Harbinger Publications.

In order to communicate assertively, you need to know how to make a simple request. Rather than demanding something, it can be helpful to calmly and politely request it.

There are four components to a request:

1. A brief justification—explain briefly what the issue is and why you're making the request
2. A softening statement—establish yourself as a reasonable, polite person by using this type of statement. Examples: "I'd appreciate it if…..", "Would you mind…..", "Can you please….."
3. A direct and specific question—simply and calmly state what you want, without blaming or accusing the other person. Use a matter-of-fact tone
4. An appreciation statement: this makes the other person feel appreciated and valued, and also makes him/her more likely to follow your request.

Examples of requests:

It's really hot in here. Would you mind turning on the fan? I'd really appreciate it.

I get nervous when you drive so fast. Would you mind slowing down a little bit? I really appreciate your understanding.

I am exhausted and it's a bit loud in here. It would be really helpful if you could turn down the volume of the television. Thanks so much.

Practice Exercise

Write a request for each of the following scenarios, using the four components listed above.

Asking a family member to do you a favor:

_____

_____

_____

_____

_____

_____

Asking a restaurant employee to bring you a drink:

_____

_____

_____

_____

_____

_____

_____

Asking a co-worker to help you with a task:

_____

_____

_____

_____

_____

_____

_____

Asking your boss for a day off:

_____

_____

_____

_____

_____

_____

_____

BARRIERS TO LISTENING

Good conflict resolution involves listening as well as assertively expressing your own thoughts and feelings. Listening is not always easy. We are often so focused on making our own point that we forget to listen to what the other person is saying. Here are some additional barriers to listening that may get in the way of conflict resolution:

- ✓ Shaming, Ridiculing, or Labeling
- ✓ Withdrawing, Distracting, Humoring, or Changing the Subject
- ✓ Warning or Threatening
- ✓ Ordering, Directing, or Commanding
- ✓ Lecturing or Arguing
- ✓ Moralizing or Preaching,
- ✓ Judging, Criticizing, or Blaming
- ✓ Agreeing, Approving, or Praising
- ✓ Interpreting or Analyzing

Which of these barriers to listening is most relevant to you?

_____

_____

_____

_____

_____

_____

How can you be a better listener?

_____

_____

_____

_____

_____

_____

Practice Exercise:

Choose a partner. One person will be the speaker and the other will be the listener. The speaker should spend just a couple of minutes talking about him/herself (interests, hobbies, job, family background, etc). The listener will practice listening to what the other person says. Don't interrupt, just listen! At the end of the exercise, the listener will repeat what he/she heard to the speaker. Check with the speaker for accuracy. Did the listener hear correctly? Did the speaker feel heard and understood? Then, switch roles and repeat the exercise.

PICK YOUR BATTLES

It is natural and common to have disagreements with other people. After all, everybody has their own perspectives, opinions, and beliefs. Sometimes, it is important to stand up for yourself. But other times, it may be wise to let go of your feelings of hurt/anger rather than addressing them. While there is no clear answer for which battles are worth fighting and which are not, it can be useful to consider what issues are really important to you, and which are minor annoyances that you would benefit from simply accepting.

Write down an example of a time that you were emotional about a situation and it ended up making your life more difficult. Were you rational or irrational?

_____

_____

_____

_____

_____

_____

_____

_____

_____

_____

_____

_____

_____

_____

_____

_____

_____

_____

SELF-ESTEEM

Self-esteem is a term in psychology to reflect a person's overall evaluation or appraisal of his or her own worth. Low self-esteem affects both males and females. Although self-esteem is rarely discussed as a male issue, men and boys are also affected by low self-esteem. Also note that there are those that use substances to mask self-esteem issues.

How does someone with low self-esteem behave?

_____

_____

_____

_____

_____

_____

How does someone with healthy self-esteem behave?

_____

_____

_____

_____

_____

_____

What is the difference between healthy self-esteem and arrogance?

_____

_____

_____

_____

_____

_____

Sometimes those with low self-esteem try to bully, abuse, or talk down to others. Why do you think they do this? Have you ever experienced this? If so, how did this affect you or others?

_____

_____

_____

_____

_____

_____

How do you deal with bullies at the workplace and in your personal life?

_____

_____

_____

_____

_____

Strategies to Improve Self-Esteem

✓ Pursue easy goals

Start with something you can accomplish easily. When we achieve small successes, it builds our confidence and momentum to go after bigger goals.

✓ Socialize

Get out of the house and practice your communication and interpersonal skills. Don't be afraid to engage in conversations. Others may be just as nervous as we are and do not express it. We are not alone. Some people are magicians and we only see what they allow us to see.

✓ Face your fears

It is important for us to face our fears so we can grow. By repeatedly facing our fears our irrational beliefs diminish and we gain confidence and courage.

✓ Build on your strengths

Do things on a regular basis that comes natural for you. Doing things that you are good at reinforces belief in your abilities and strengths. You can also add to your skills by taking advanced coursework or certification training in your field of study.

✓ Stop comparing yourself to others

Stop comparing yourself to other people. Low self-esteem stems from the feeling of being inferior. For example, if you were the only person in the world, do you think you could have low self-esteem? Self-esteem only comes into the picture when there are other people around us and we perceive that we are inferior. Don't worry about what your neighbor is doing. Accept that it'll serve you more to just go down your own path at your own pace rather than to compare yourself.

✓ Know thyself

Know who you are and what you need to improve on. Your self-esteem is based on the major categories of your life. Write down all the major categories of your life (e.g., health, finance, relationships, etc.). Then rate yourself on a scale of 1-10 in each area. Work on the lowest numbered category first. Each area affects the other areas. The more you build up each area of your life, the higher your overall self-esteem.

✓ Create a vision of yourself

Use your imagination and create an image of yourself as the confident and

self-assured person you aspire to become. When you are this person, how will you feel? How will others perceive you? What does your body language look like?

How will you talk? Feel the emotions, experiences, and daydream about your ideal life.

✓ Help others achieve their goals

Helping others achieve their goals can be fulfilling. It puts a smile on their face and can make you feel good as well. Plus if you help them with their goals, maybe they will help you with your goals.

✓ Create a plan

Having a goal is not enough. You need to have an action plan. Get moving and follow the steps that you need to take to achieve your goals.

✓ Get motivated

Be purpose driven. Have a reason why you are doing something. Associate yourself with people or things that inspire you. If you desire to be motivated, use this formula: High Emotion + Strong Purpose = Motivation

✓ Improve self-talk

Sometimes we have internal thoughts that are negative and irrational. We have to manage our self-talk and reinforce positive thoughts that improve our perspective. Internally, we can say good things about ourselves and build a positive image.

✓ Be positive

There are many people that allow negative energy to transfer into their lives. Know that it is okay to smile and people are attracted to happy people. Do not allow negative people to transfer their energy into you. Just because they are mad does not mean that you have to be. You are in control of your perceptions. There are no benefits to being negative.

PERSONAL ADVICE

Imagine that you are five years in the future and you have to write a letter to your present self. What advice would you give?

_____

_____

_____

_____

_____

_____

_____

_____

_____

_____

_____

_____

_____

_____

_____

_____

_____

_____

_____

_____

_____

_____

CULTURAL IDENTITY

Our cultural identities influence who we are and how we see the world. They influence our beliefs, how we interact with others, and how we manage our anger. Understanding your cultural identify is an important step in understanding why you may have experienced difficulties with anger management.

What is your cultural identity? Consider your race/ethnicity, religion, geographic location, primary language, any disabilities, and other factors that influence your perceptions of the world.

_____

_____

_____

_____

_____

_____

_____

_____

_____

What challenges have you faced when dealing with people whose culture differs from yours?

_____

_____

_____

_____

_____

_____

_____

_____

EXPLORING BIASES

Our view of the world is never completely accurate. We each have our own biases that influence the way that we perceive the world around us. Based on our personal experiences, we hold certain beliefs about people whose race, culture, gender, sexual orientation, and religion differ from our own. When we make generalizations, we are showing our biases. Our biases can contribute to unrealistic anger, if we are negatively labeling people or making unfair assumptions about them, While it is impossible to completely get rid of our biases, it is important that we acknowledge and understand them so that we can choose our behaviors more consciously and with increased awareness, rather than acting on our biases.

It may feel uncomfortable to admit some of your biases, but acknowledging them is a necessary step toward better understanding yourself and how your actions may be influenced by your biases. Please be as honest as possible when answering the following questions.

What are some biases that you have based on race/ethnicity? Consider beliefs that you have about the characteristics of specific cultures or races.

_____

_____

_____

_____

In your opinion, how do men and women differ? What can men do that women can't? Do you believe that men are superior to women, or vice versa?

_____

_____

_____

_____

What are your beliefs about people from specific religions, such as Christianity, Judaism, and Islam?

_____

_____

_____

_____

What are your beliefs about members of the LGBT community?

_____

_____

_____

_____

What biases do you hold toward people who have a disability of some type?

_____

_____

_____

_____

What beliefs do you hold about people who identify as Democrats? What beliefs do you hold about people who identify as Republicans?

_____

_____

_____

_____

_____

_____

_____

_____

How have the above biases affected your interactions with people? Can you think of a time when you treated people differently based on your biases?

_____

_____

_____

_____

FORGIVENESS

Forgiveness is one of the hardest things to do, but it is also extremely important. Letting go of the past and removing resentment is healthy. There are no benefits to holding on to grudges and past hurts. It's like driving a car while looking through the rearview mirror. Eventually, you will crash.

Who do you need to forgive and why?

Family Friends Co-workers   Spouse Children   Yourself Do you forgive and forget? Or is it better to forgive but remember?

_____

_____

_____

_____

_____

_____

Is making amends important to you? If so, who do you need to say sorry to, and why?

_____

_____

_____

_____

_____

_____

What does true forgiveness look, act, and sound like?

_____

_____

_____

_____

After you forgive someone, does that mean you should still associate yourself with them?

It is important to note that forgiveness is not the same as approval. You can forgive somebody without implying that their actions were acceptable. Forgiveness serves to benefit you, by allowing you to move forward and let go of negative feelings that may hold you back.

LIVING BY PRINCIPLES

It is important to have principles. Principles are the governors of your values and protect the things that you care about the most. The principles that you create will help you when you need to make tough decisions.

Values

Freedom

Principle: I do not hang out with people who sell or use drugs.

This protects my freedom, life, and family.

Career

Principle: I attend trainings quarterly to improve my skill level.

This helps my career and shows that I am committed.

Reputation

Principle: I have a strong work ethic and provide quality service.

This protects my reputation and increases my earning potential.

List the things that you value.

1._____

2._____

3._____

4._____

Now write down **principles** that protect those values.

1._____

_____

_____

2._____

_____

_____

3._____

_____

4.

VALUES

Source: Hayes, S. C. (2005). Get out of your mind & into your life. Oakland, CA: New Harbinger Publications, Inc.

Values are the things that are most important to us in our lives. Although we all make mistakes and behave in ways that are not in line with our morals and ideals, values provide a path that we aspire to follow. Identifying your own values can help you get a better idea of who you are and want you want in life.

What are some of the things that you value most?

_____

_____

_____

_____

_____

How do you want to be remembered?

_____

_____

_____

_____

_____

Write down your values in each of the following domains:

Marriage/intimate relationship:

_____

_____

_____

_____

_____

Parenting:

_____
_____
_____
_____
_____

Family relationships (other than intimate partners and parenting)

_____
_____
_____
_____
_____

Friendships:

_____
_____
_____
_____
_____

Career:

_____
_____
_____
_____
_____

Education/training/personal growth:

_____
_____

_____

_____

_____

Recreation:

_____

_____

_____

_____

_____

Spirituality:

_____

_____

_____

_____

_____

Citizenship:

_____

_____

_____

_____

_____

Health:

_____

_____

_____

_____

BELIEF AND SELF-IMAGE

What is your overall view of yourself physically, emotionally, and intellectually?

Physically I am:

_____   _____

_____   _____

_____   _____

_____   _____

Emotionally I am:

_____   _____

_____   _____

_____   _____

_____   _____

Intellectually I am:

_____   _____

_____   _____

_____   _____

_____   _____

Spiritually I am:

_____   _____

_____   _____

_____   _____

_____   _____

Write down a list of "shoulds" that you have based on your family, friends, culture, spirituality, media, music, school system, and any other areas. Which of these beliefs are rational and which are irrational? Place an "R" next the beliefs that you think are rational and an "I" next to the beliefs that you deem irrational. Place an "X" next to the statements that describe who you are currently.

		R or I	I am
Example:	I should be skinny	R	X
	I should be perfect	I	
	I should be married by now	I	
	I should get all A's		R

I should _____ ____ ____

I should _____ ____ ____

I should _____ ____ ____

I should _____ ____ ____

I should _____ ____ ____

I should _____ ____ ____

I should _____ ____ ____

I should _____ ____ ____

I should _____ ____ ____

I should _____ ____ ____

Write down as many great things about yourself that you can think of in the next 2 minutes.

_____   _____

_____   _____

_____   _____

_____   _____

_____   _____

_____   _____

Write down as many not-so-great things about yourself that you can think of in the next 2 minutes.

_____   _____

_____   _____

_____   _____

_____   _____

_____   _____

_____   _____

Now analyze your two lists. Was it more difficult to write one list than the other? Which list is longer? Why do you think that is?

_____

_____

_____

_____

_____

Write a list of things that people have told you about yourself. Place an "X" next to the statements that you either agree or disagree with.

Example:	Agree	Disagree
I am an excellent writer.	___X___	
I am lazy.	___X___	
_____	_____	_____
_____	_____	_____
_____	_____	_____
_____	_____	_____
_____	_____	_____
_____	_____	_____

Write a list of things that you believe people think about you. Place an "X" next to the statements that you either agree or disagree with.

Finish the following statement:

People believe that I am:	Agree	Disagree
_____	_____	_____
_____	_____	_____
_____	_____	_____
_____	_____	_____
_____	_____	_____
_____	_____	_____

CHALLENGING NEGATIVE SELF-TALK

Source: Martin, B. (2016). Challenging negative self-talk. Retrieved from

http://psychcentral.com/lib/challenging-negative-self-talk/

In the above exercise, you identified some beliefs about how you "should" be, which are influenced by your family, friends, culture, and other factors. While it is important to have ideals that we aspire to, focusing too much on "shoulds" can leave you feeling like you are not good enough, which in turn can prevent you from making positive changes in your life. If you find yourself thinking badly about yourself, using negative labels to describe yourself, or engaging in other negative self-talk, it can be useful to challenge those problematic thoughts so that you don't get stuck in a cycle of negativity.

What are some irrational negative beliefs that you hold about yourself? (You can use the irrational beliefs you listed in the above exercise, as well as any others that come to mind.)

_____

_____

_____

_____

_____

_____

_____

_____

Here are some ways to challenge those negative beliefs:

- Reality testing—Consider the evidence for/against a specific belief. Identify whether the belief is rational or irrational. For example, a belief that you should be perfect is irrational because nobody is perfect.
- Identify alternative beliefs—Are there other beliefs that may be more rational or helpful? What would you say to a friend who held this belief about him/herself? How might the belief change if you were to maintain a more positive perspective about yourself?
- Maintain perspective—It is common to build things up in our head to make them a bigger deal than they really are. Consider whether the situation is really as bad as you are making it out to be. In 5 years, will you still hold this belief?

ACCEPTANCE

We all have flaws, and we all make mistakes. Sometimes, our negative beliefs about ourselves may hold some truth. In that case, it is best to acknowledge and accept our flaws so that we can move forward in a healthy way. There are some things that we can change about ourselves, such as our behaviors and beliefs. On the other hand, there are some things that we can't change, such as aspects of our physical appearance and other qualities that we were born with. When we can't change something, we can benefit from accepting it.

Consider the list of not so good things about yourself that you created earlier when answering the following questions:

Which of the not so good things can you change?

_____

_____

_____

_____

_____

_____

_____

_____

Which are most important to change?

_____

_____

_____

_____

_____

_____

_____

_____

List at least 3 things that you can do to make positive changes in those areas. Be specific.

_____

_____

_____

_____

_____

_____

_____

Which of the not so good things that you identified can't be changed?

_____

_____

_____

_____

_____

_____

_____

Can you accept those things about yourself?

_____

_____

_____

_____

_____

_____

_____

FAMILY DRAMA

Our early family experiences have great influence over our adult identities. The relationships that we have with our parents or other caregivers can lay the foundation for future relationships throughout our lives. Even as an adult, your relationship with your family can cause stress and tension. It is important to understand how our families have shaped who we are, and how they continue to affect us currently.

How has your family affected your emotions?

_____

_____

_____

_____

_____

How has your family influenced your relationships with others?

_____

_____

_____

_____

Which family member can "push your buttons" the most? What do they do?

_____

_____

_____

_____

_____

What strategies do other people use in your family to deal with the person mentioned on the previous page?

_____

_____

_____

_____

_____

What role do you play in your family conflicts? How do your behaviors affect the experience of having your buttons pushed? How can you change the effect that it has on you?

_____

_____

_____

_____

_____

How have family secrets affected your life positively or negatively?

_____

_____

_____

_____

_____

Is denial about substance, sexual, verbal, or physical abuse acceptable within the family? Should this history of behavior be hidden from family members? Why or why not?

_____

_____

_____

_____

_____

Should accomplishments, awards, promotions, or scholarships be hidden from family members?

_____

_____

_____

_____
_____
_____
_____

How can you improve your family?

_____
_____
_____
_____
_____

Is family something that you value? If so, in what ways do you show that you value your family?

_____
_____
_____
_____
_____

Are you improving your family or are you keeping the family drama alive?

_____
_____
_____
_____
_____

Would you raise your children the same way your parents raised you? If not, what changes would you make?

_____
_____
_____
_____
_____

LET IT GO

What is the purpose of holding on to the past?

_____

_____

_____

_____

_____

Where does "holding on to the past" get you?

_____

_____

_____

_____

_____

Is your past affecting you presently? If so, how?

_____

_____

_____

_____

_____

Does holding on to negative things in your past benefit you in any way?

_____

_____

_____

Seriously, does being negative or pessimistic lead to positive results?

_____

_____

_____

_____

_____

If no, why do people continue to do it?

_____

_____

_____

_____

_____

What are the characteristics of victims?

_____

_____

_____

_____

_____

Do those characteristics describe you? Would you like to be held in eternal bondage by your past?

_____

_____

_____

_____

_____

_____

_____

_____

_____

_____

What is the best way to get over your past?

_____

_____

_____

_____

_____

DELAYED GRATIFICATION

Those who practice delayed gratification usually have less issues with impulse-control and have been known to live longer, more fulfilled lives.

Impulsivity can be a serious problem. When we give into our urges without thinking them through, we can end up in trouble. Although you may want to fulfill your urges right away, there is great value in being able to delay gratification so

that you do not act without thinking

_____

_____

_____

_____

_____

How has instant gratification affected your life?

_____

_____

_____

_____

_____

What are the benefits of delayed gratification?

_____

_____

_____

_____

_____

_____

What are the cons of instant gratification?

_____

_____

_____

_____

_____

Are fast things good for you? Please explain.

_____

_____

_____

_____

_____

Do good things come to those who wait? Please explain.

_____

_____

_____

_____

_____

How can delayed gratification improve your life?

_____

_____

_____

_____

_____

FEAR

Many people are controlled by fear. These fears can manifest into anger and impulse-control problems. Many express their anger because they don't want to accept a foreseeable consequence. FEAR is irrational and it stands for: false existence appearing real.

What are you really afraid of? Be honest.

_____
_____
_____
_____

What is your greatest fear?

_____
_____
_____
_____

What has fear stopped you from doing?

_____
_____
_____
_____

What benefits do you gain from confronting your fears?

_____
_____
_____
_____

CONSEQUENCES OF POOR ANGER MANAGEMENT

- ✓ Expulsion from school
- ✓ Loss of time
- ✓ Loss of respect
- ✓ Loss of relationships
- ✓ Added stress
- ✓ Probation
- ✓ Community Service
- ✓ Loss of freedom
- ✓ Loss of money
- ✓ Health problems
- ✓ Loss of professional licenses
- ✓ Public humiliation
- ✓ Diminished reputation
- ✓ Loss of property
- ✓ Criminal record
- ✓ Court fees, fines, etc.
- ✓ Employment loss
- ✓ Loss of citizenship/residency
- ✓ Embarrassment
- ✓ Guilt
- ✓ Trauma

FINANCIAL CONSEQUENCES

Fines $_____

Income lost from not working $_____

Legal Fees (Probation/Court/Lawyer) $_____

Anger Management Evaluation $_____

Anger Management Classes $_____

Childcare $_____

Gas $_____

Food bought while taking classes $_____

Loss of wages $_____

Repair bills or restitution $_____

TOTAL MONEY LOST $_____

Hours in court Hours in probation   _____

Hours doing community service   _____

Hours in jail   _____

Hours in class   _____

Other hours lost   _____

TOTAL TIME LOST   _____

TIME x HOURLY WAGE = VALUE OF TIME LOST

_____X $ _____   =$ _____

VALUE OF TIME LOST $_____

VALUE OF TIME LOST + TOTAL MONEY LOSS= $_____

IS IT WORTH IT?

_____

_____

_____

TRUTHFULNESS

Honesty is an important quality in relationships not just with others, but also with ourselves. While everybody is dishonest from time to time, addressing conflicts in an open and honest way is crucial for a healthy relationship. Let's explore some of your ideas about honesty.

Can women handle the truth? Why or why not?

_____

_____

_____

_____

_____

_____

Can men handle the truth? Why or why not?

_____

_____

_____

_____

_____

_____

What are things that women lie about?

_____

_____

_____

_____

_____

_____

What are things that men lie about?

_____

_____

_____

_____

_____

Who are better liars? Women or men?

_____

_____

_____

_____

_____

How do women lie differently than men? How do they cover it up? What tactics do they use?

_____

_____

_____

_____

_____

Do you respect liars? Why or why not?

_____

_____

_____

_____

_____

Do you lie to yourself? If so, why?

_____

_____

_____

_____

_____

_____

What is the purpose of a lie?

_____

_____

_____

_____

_____

_____

How have lies hurt you in the past?

_____

_____

_____

_____

Strip away your ego, defenses, and lies you tell yourself. Truly, who are you?

_____

_____

_____

_____

DECISION TREE

In life, we are required to make a lot of decisions, both big and small. Each choice we make will have a ripple effect on many different aspects of our life that we may have failed to consider. This is why it is very important to evaluate our choices in order to create the best possible outcomes.

Creating a decision tree helps you see the possible ripple effects of your choices.

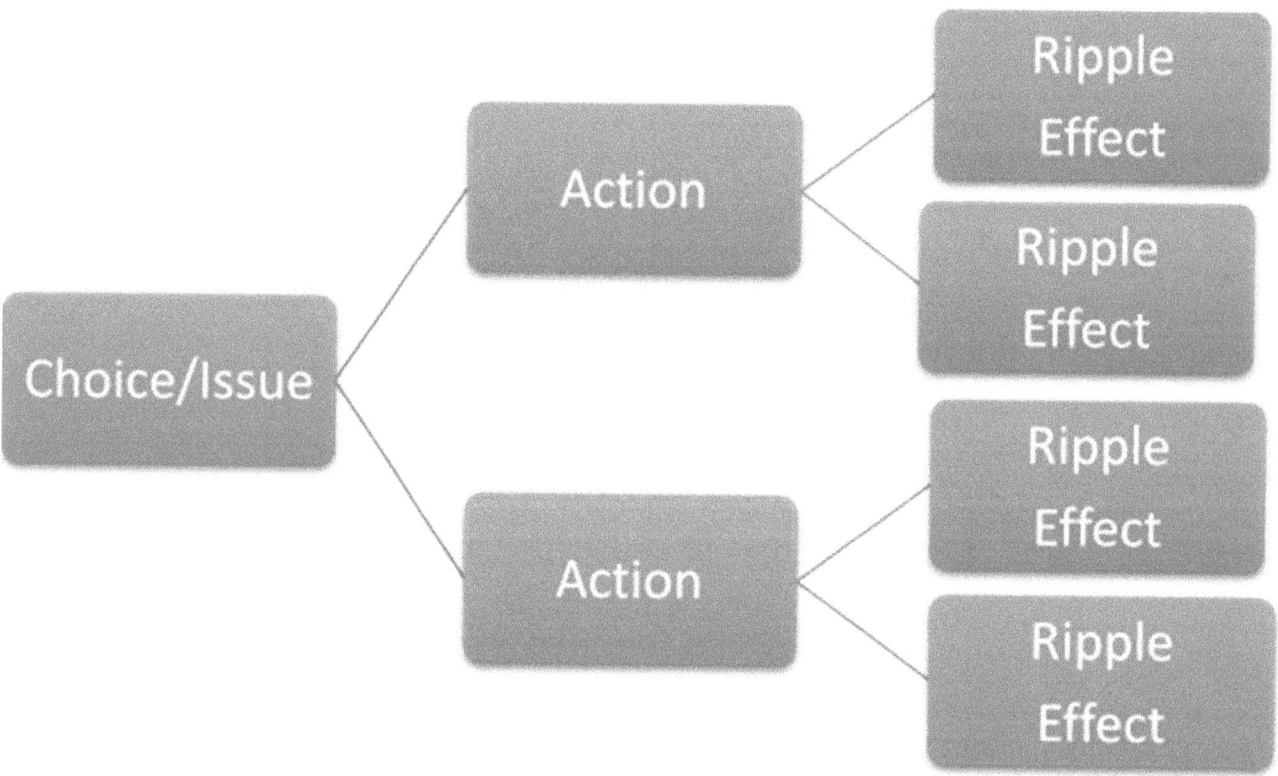

Sample Decision Tree

Please create your own decision tree and evaluate your choices on this page.

SELF-AWARENESS

Knowing yourself is important. When you are self-aware, you are better able to understand your triggers, fears, reactions, and emotions so that you can gain more control over your behaviors. Self-awareness allows you to respond to a situation thoughtfully, rather than simply reacting to it.

What makes you feel happy, relaxed, and fulfilled?

_____

_____

_____

_____

_____

_____

What are the top three distractions or weaknesses that keep you from achieving your goals? How will you remove these weaknesses or distractions?

_____

_____

_____

_____

_____

_____

What are your strengths? Are there other skills that you need to develop? If so, what are they?

_____

_____

_____

_____

_____

_____

Pretend that you were told by your doctor that you had five years to live. How would you change your life? Would you do anything differently?

_____

_____

_____

_____

_____

_____

What do you want to be known for? What kind of legacy will you leave behind?

_____

_____

_____

_____

_____

_____

Describe the characteristics of your ideal mate. What kind of personality does he/she have? What are his/her physical characteristics? What are deal breakers for you?

Personality	Physical Features	Deal Breakers	Other

What was the best birthday you ever had? What did you do and who was there?

_____

_____

_____

_____

_____

_____

Who do you admire and respect? What qualities do they have and what do you need to do to get those same qualities?

_____

_____

_____

_____

_____

1. Name: _____ Relationship: _____

Qualities: _____

2. Name: _____ _____Relationship: _____

Qualities: _____

If you could be any fictional character, who would you be and why?

_____

_____

_____

_____

_____

If you had a million dollars right now, how would you spend or invest it? Be specific.

_____

_____

_____

_____

CREDIT

So what is credit anyway? In essence, credit is any form of delayed payment. It allows one party (the debtor or borrower) to receive money, goods, or services from another party (the creditor or lender) without having to pay up front.

Instead there is an agreement based on trust that the borrower will either pay or return the materials (or other materials of equal value) at a later date. The cost of credit comes in the form of a predetermined rate of interest that is applied to the amount borrowed and will accrue until the debt has been paid.

Common forms of credit include:

Mortgages

Personal loans

Credit Cards

Store Cards

Automobile loans

Credit bureaus collect information from various sources regarding your borrowing and bill-paying habits and create a report based on these findings. A credit score is a number that represents your credit worthiness. It is formulated based on your

credit report. The most common credit scores are FICO scores. FICO scores range from 300 – 850. The higher the score, the better your credit. Your credit score is used to determine whether you are worthy of credit, to determine interest rates, and assess your ability to pay back loans. In essence, your past behavior is used to predict your future behavior. Because credit is based on trust and your previous financial behavior, it is very important to create a flawless track record of bill paying activity.

1. Do you know your credit score? If so, what is it?

_____

_____

_____

_____

2. When was the last time you checked your credit score and credit report?

_____

_____

_____

_____

_____

3. Do you typically pay your bills on time? Why or why not?

_____

_____

_____

_____

_____

4. How many lines of credit do you have open (credit cards, loans, etc.)?

_____

_____

_____

_____

_____

5. Are your credit cards maxed out? If so, why?

_____

_____

_____

_____

_____

6. Do you pay the minimum amount allowed? If so, why?

_____

_____

_____

_____

_____

The United States has 3
national credit bureaus:

   Equifax

   Experian

   TransUnion

7. How soon do you think you will be able to pay off your credit cards?

_____

_____

_____

_____

8. Do you have a plan in place to pay off your debts? If so, what is it?

_____

_____

_____

9. How can you improve your credit? (FYI, having no credit is bad credit)

_____

_____

_____

_____

PERSONAL BUDGET

Many people become angry, depressed, or stressed out due to poor financial management. On this page, create a monthly budget for yourself based on your current income.

Mortgage/Rent:

_____

Utilities:

_____

Groceries:

_____

Insurance:

_____

Cell Phone:

_____

Internet:

_____

Credit Card:

_____

Entertainment/Self Care:

_____

Clothing:

_____

Gas:

_____

Misc.:

_____

Savings:

_____

Money in	- Money out	= Money left

Notes:

_____

_____

_____

_____

AMYGDALA HIJACKING

Amygdala hijack describes a situation when a person responds inappropriately based on emotional rather than intellectual factors. The amygdala is the emotional center of the human brain and makes quick responses when a person is threatened. An inappropriate emotional response to a perceived threat is called an amygdala hijack.

The process for the amygdala's response is to: Act→ Feel→Think or Feel→Act→Think.

We want you to: Think→Act→Feel

The amygdala is the part of the brain that protects us from threats. It is considered to be used as a survival mechanism during extreme stimulus or triggers. The prefrontal cortex is the part of the brain where conscious control and decision making processes occur.

During low to moderate stressful events, the prefrontal cortex will calm amygdala down and consider the pros and cons of taking actions. When the stimulus is extreme, the amygdala will shut down the prefrontal cortex function and take over to protect us from threats.

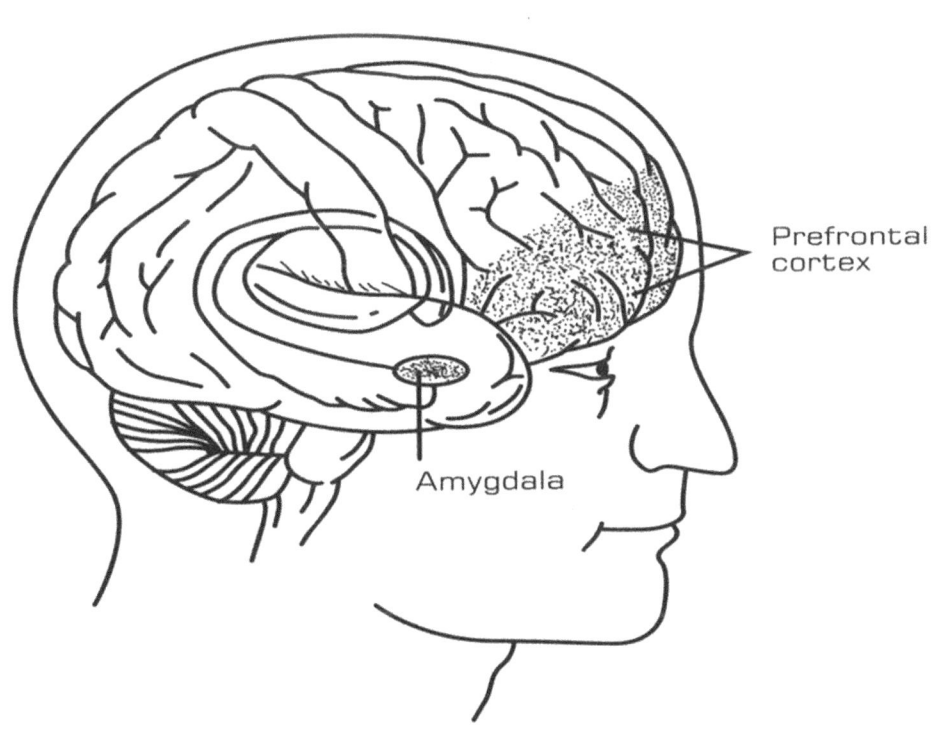

Unfortunately many people who suffer from chronic anger perceive low to moderate events as extreme events and activate un-necessary flight or fight responses. "Flight or fight" refers to building up energy to run away, or building up energy to fight. Continuous activation of this process can lead to chronic health problems and negative life experiences.

DECISION-MAKING SCENARIOS

Behavior is developed through our values, principles and the consequences of our actions. Each decision or choice that you make has a ripple effect. We would like for you to practice your decision-making skills while being exposed to emotionally-charged scenarios. There are no right or wrong answers. We just want you to practice making decisions while being emotionally charged.

If you want to get better at singing, public speaking, driving a car, painting, or doing some other skill, you need to practice. People who live the best lives make the best decisions. We want you to make the best decisions for your life.

On the next page, there is a series of scenarios for you to evaluate. Please have a response for each scenario listed. Please keep it real and don't give answers that you think your group or counselor want to hear. Remember this is a judgment-free zone.

Scenario # 1

School is about to start and you just bought some new school clothes for your daughter. While she waits at the bus stop, a neighborhood bully rips her clothes and harasses her. Your daughter reports this back to you and you find out that this bully's parent is your supervisor at your job. How do you handle this situation?

_____

_____

_____

_____

Scenario # 2

Your mom is single and she is dating someone who is the same age as you. They invite you to dinner where he proposes to her and she gladly accepts. They have been only dating for a month. Later that evening, he comes to you and asks for your blessing and support of his marriage to your mom. How do you handle this situation?

_____

_____

_____

_____

Scenario # 3

You are a mother/father of three children. You're offered a spot on a popular reality show. The pay is $200,000 per episode. The show is very popular and known for having a lot of fights, arguments, and undignified behavior. In order to be on the show you must behave the same way (i.e., argue and fight, tell the world all your deep dark secrets, sexualize yourself, let people disrespect you, disrespect others and show the worst sides of yourself). What would you do?

_____

_____

_____

_____

_____

Scenario # 4

You're watching the news and you see video footage of a man that is wanted by the police for murdering a woman and burning her body on the side of the road near your house. The man looks exactly like your brother. Just a week before, on the night of the murder, your brother came to your house looking worried and asking for a gas can. Although you didn't give him your gas can, you noticed later on that it was missing. What would you do?

_____

_____

_____

_____

Scenario # 5

You are at a family gathering and your cousin has brought his new girlfriend. You notice that he is being verbally abusive to her (i.e., calling her out of her name, saying disrespectful things and threatening to beat her up). What do you do?

_____

_____

_____

_____

Scenario # 6

You are on probation and your supervisor needs a ride home. He uses cocaine on a regular basis and is known to have cocaine on him at all times. Do you give him a ride home?

_____

_____

_____

_____

Scenario # 7

You are struggling financially and your neighbor is "getting over" because she is getting disability, food stamps, and a tax return for three kids that are not hers.

Plus she has a babysitting business next door and is not licensed by the state to run a daycare.

1. Do you report her?
2. Do you blackmail her to get a cut of her money?
3. Do you ignore the situation and mind your business?
4. Other _____

Scenario # 8

You get laid off from work and receive your final check. With this check you now have a total of $800 left to your name to pay your $700 rent, $300 car note, and

$200 in utility bills. It is your daughter's sixth birthday next week. How do you handle this situation? What will be your strategy?

_____

_____

_____

_____

Scenario # 9

You are hanging out at your friend's house watching football and he decides to invite more people over to watch the game. These are all of the people that you used to drink and drug with before you entered treatment. How will you handle this situation?

_____

_____

_____

_____

Scenario # 10

You and your co-worker were given a joint project to complete but your co-worker was lazy and you ended up doing all the work. When it was time to present to your boss your co-worker took over the presentation and made it seem like they were the leader on it. Your boss then praised your co-worker and said nothing to you.

How do you handle this situation?

_____

_____

_____

_____

_____

MINDSET MAINTENANCE

✓ Know your triggers and stay away from them.
✓ Find alternate ways to cope.
✓ Go to counseling for un-resolved issues like grief, depression, anger, anxiety, substance use, or a gambling or sex addiction.
✓ Engage in activities that improve your mood (manage your emotions).
✓ Do positive things that you used to enjoy that you don't do now (nostalgia, music, hobbies, old television shows).
✓ Try something new and gain exposure to exciting things that interest you.
✓ Resolve personal issues with family, friends and coworkers.
✓ Be assertive and do not be afraid to tell people "no."
✓ Be aware and adjust your behavior patterns.
✓ Stay away from negative influences.
✓ Develop an action plan to improve emotionally, physically, and financially.
✓ Understand the long-term consequences of your actions and how it will affect you personally, professionally, and emotionally.
✓ Practice delayed gratification.
✓ Create a budget for yourself and only buy what you need and save for the future.
✓ When you have the urge to engage in negative behaviors, know that you have a choice. You are not on auto-pilot and you can control your behavior.
✓ Go to school and improve your marketability by earning a degree, trade, or license in a specialized field. Work on professional goals.
✓ Exercise regularly and try to get sunlight as much as possible to increase endorphins.
✓ Do positive things and engage in legal experiences that make you happy.
✓ Develop a relapse prevention plan. Pre-plan on how you are going to respond to stress, anxiety, failure, and mistakes in a positive manner that lead to long-term success.
✓ Go to church and get spiritual guidance.

TIME MANAGEMENT

Goals   Priority   Deadline

1. _____   _____   _____

2. _____   _____   _____

3. _____   _____   _____

4. _____   _____   _____

5. _____   _____   _____

Time   Activity   Time   Activity

_____   _____   _____   _____

Monday

_____   _____   _____   _____

_____   _____   _____   _____

_____   _____   _____   _____

_____   _____   _____   _____

Time   Activity   Time   Activity

_____   _____   _____   _____

Tuesday

_____   _____   _____   _____

_____   _____   _____   _____

_____   _____   _____   _____

_____   _____   _____   _____

Time   Activity   Time   Activity

_____   _____   _____   _____

Wednesday

_____   _____   _____   _____

_____   _____   _____   _____

_____   _____   _____   _____

_____   _____   _____   _____

Time   Activity   Time   Activity

_____   _____   _____   _____

Thursday

_____   _____   _____   _____

_____   _____   _____   _____

_____   _____   _____   _____

                 _____   _____   _____

Time   Activity   Time   Activity

_____   _____   _____   _____

Friday

_____   _____   _____   _____

_____   _____   _____   _____

_____   _____   _____   _____

_____   _____   _____   _____

Time   Activity   Time   Activity

_____   _____   _____   _____

Saturday

_____   _____   _____   _____
_____   _____   _____   _____
_____   _____   _____   _____
_____   _____   _____   _____

Time   Activity   Time   Activity

_____   _____   _____   _____

Sunday

_____   _____   _____   _____
_____   _____   _____   _____
_____   _____   _____   _____
_____   _____   _____   _____

Time   Activity   Time   Activity

_____   _____   _____   _____

SETTING GOALS

Many people are angry, depressed, or dissatisfied with life because they do not pursue their dreams or desires. This is not going to be you. Setting goals is an important part of personal development. In order to improve ourselves and our

lives, we need to know what we are striving for.

Write a list of short-term and long-term goals that you would like to accomplish.

_____

_____

_____

_____

_____

Transform your list of goals into SMART goals by answering the following questions. Start with the first goal listed above.

Goal:

_____

_____

_____

Specific: What specifically do you want to do?

_____

_____

_____

_____

Measurable: How will you measure your success? How much? How many?

_____

_____

_____

_____

_____

Attainable: Is it in your power to accomplish this goal?

_____

_____

_____

_____

_____

Relevant: Is this goal consistent with your other goals and plans.

_____

_____

_____

_____

_____

Time-bound: What is the established deadline that will create a reasonable sense of urgency for you to complete the goal?

_____

_____

_____

_____

_____

SMART Goal:

_____

_____

_____

PROFESSIONAL DEVELOPMENT

What can you specialize in that makes you different from the crowd? What special skill, niche, or talent can you develop that will put you in demand?

What special skills and talents do you already possess? Consider skills that you have been trained on, as well as natural, innate abilities that you may have.

_____

_____

_____

_____

_____

Homework Assignment:

Go on the internet and search for careers that require a special skill or training that you would be willing to commit to. Look for something that most people are not doing or thinking about. Look for apprenticeship and certification programs. Do not be discouraged if it requires you to jump through a lot of hoops. This element is created to weed out competition and the people who are not serious.

Sample Careers:

Food Stylist

Deep Sea Welder

Horse Exerciser

Trauma Cleanup

Polygraph Examiner

Foley Artist List the careers that you are interested in:

Millwright Glass Blower

Cremator

Mediator

Elevator Inspector

Locomotive Engineer

_____

_____

_____

_____

What was cool in High School is not cool in adulthood. Many people learn this lesson the hard way and end up being angry due to regret. Successful people tend to sacrifice time, money, and their wants to gain what they need for long-term success. They choose to give up toxic lifestyles, friends, and environments to live a fulfilled life. Others choose another path and end up suffering throughout adulthood because of poor decision making. When their back is against the wall, or when a crisis emerges, they have to rely on doing something that can potentially put them in a worse situation than before. Who will you decide to be? Will you be the person who chooses to sacrifice their wants for their needs, or the person who sacrifices their needs for their wants?

What is the difference between a want and a need?

_____

_____

_____

_____

_____

What is your ideal career and what steps do you need to take today to get there?

_____

_____

_____

_____

_____

Who or what do you need to remove from your life to achieve this goal?

_____

_____

_____

_____

_____

In your city or state who is the leader in your field of choice? Would you allow them to mentor you?

_____

_____

_____

_____

_____

What is your life's purpose? If you do not know, consider gaining exposure to different people, places, and things so you can find out what you're really good at. You could be a natural violin player but wouldn't even know it because you have never touched a violin.

_____

_____

_____

_____

_____

What lifestyle choices do you need to give up to improve your health?

_____

_____

_____

_____

_____

What sacrifices can you make right now to achieve long-term success?

_____

_____

_____

_____

_____

SELF-CARE

There are those in this world who fail to take care of themselves. Due to this, they suffer at work, have poor relationships, live shorter lives, use illegal drugs to cope, etc. It is important that we take care of ourselves. Check the things that you would like to do to improve your self-care.

_____ Massages

_____ Vacation

_____ Manicures

_____ Counseling

_____ Pedicures

_____ Improve Living Environment

_____ Facials

_____ Improve Work Environment

_____ Staycation

_____ Buy New Clothes

_____ Alone time

_____ Sleep

_____ Sunlight

_____ Read

_____ Exercise

_____ Improve Eating Habits

_____ Be in Nature

_____ Hobbies

_____ Socialize

_____ Other

Self-Care Plan

Now that you have identified some self-care activities that you are interested in, develop a more specific plan for self-care.

What activity can you commit to doing each day for self-care? It should be something that does not require a lot of time or money, so that it is feasible to practice it each day.

_____

_____

_____

_____

What activity can you do monthly for self-care? This may be something that takes more time or money than your daily activity.

_____

_____

_____

_____

_____

_____

It is important to recognize what barriers might impede you from practicing self-care. Sometimes people believe that they don't have enough to take care of themselves, or that they need to care for other people before themselves. In reality, if you do not practice adequate self-care, you are likely to suffer negative consequences which will prevent you from attending to other important areas in your life.

What barriers may prevent you from practicing self-care?

_____

_____

_____

_____

_____

_____

What can you do to ensure that you make time to take care of yourself? Who can support you in your goal of practicing self-care?

_____

_____

_____

_____

_____

_____

BELIEVE IN YOURSELF

If you do all the activities in this book and understand the concepts presented, but fail to believe in yourself, this will be a waste of your time.

This is the link in the chain that many people miss. They go after their goals, but secretly believe that they will not achieve them. They are lukewarm and passive instead of being on fire and aggressive. They lack confidence and continue to second-guess themselves due to fear and emotional baggage. You can manage your anger and you can accomplish your dreams if you believe in yourself.

Believability Scale

1   2   3   4   5   6   7   8   9   10

On a scale of one to ten, one being the lowest and ten being the highest, circle the number that represents your belief that you can be successful in managing your anger. If you circle ten, that means you are very confident. If you circle one, that means that you are not confident.

Explain why you chose the number you circled.

_____

_____

_____

_____

_____

What can you do to increase your belief?

_____

_____

_____

_____

_____

REMEMBER YOUR SUCCESSES

When times are tough, it can be challenging to remember that there were better times in the past. But everybody has been successful at something. Reflecting on your successes can help you feel more confident in your ability to make positive change in the present or future.

List some positive changes that you have made in your life.

_____

_____

_____

_____

_____

Choose one of those successes and list the steps that you took in order to make that change:

_____

_____

_____

_____

_____

_____

What factors helped you to make that change? Consider both internal factors (motivation, intelligence, etc) and external ones (support, rewards, etc).

_____

_____

_____

_____

_____

_____

What resources (internal and external) will help you to make positive changes now?

_____

_____

_____

_____

_____

ACCOUNTABILITY PARTNERS

Sometimes we need assistance in being accountable for our action or inaction. Accountability partners can help us stay on track with our goals by checking our progress. They tell us what we need to hear, not what we want to hear.

Accountability partners tell us the truth and are not enablers. They are invested in our long-term success. They can be friends, family members, or co-workers.

Write down the qualities of a great accountability partner.

_____

_____

_____

_____

_____

_____

_____

Do you feel it is important for someone to hold you accountable?

Yes or No

Write down names of potential accountability partners who you trust to hold you accountable. Be careful in who you choose. Everyone is not meant to be an accountability partner. The person you choose may have great qualities, but may not be great in holding people accountable.

Potential Accountability Partners	What qualities do they have?

GRATITUDE

Source: Morin, A. (2015). Seven scientifically proven benefits of gratitude. Retrieved from

https://www.psychologytoday.com/blog/what-mentally-strong-people-dont-do/201504/7-scientifically-proven-benefi ts-gratitude

We sometimes forget about our blessings and take them for granted. It is important to appreciate the things that we have. Even when things feel bad in your own life, there are always things to be grateful for. And focusing on gratitude has significant benefits, including improved physical and mental wellbeing, improved self-esteem, and reduced aggression.

List the things that you are thankful for.

_____   _____

_____   _____

_____   _____

_____   _____

People take care of the things that they truly appreciate. For example, if someone appreciates their car, they keep their car clean and make sure that they keep up on the maintenance. Appreciation is more than saying words. It is consists of feeling thankful and doing things that show that you are appreciative.

List the things that you can do to show your appreciation.

_____

_____

_____

_____

_____

_____

_____

_____

_____

_____

BUCKET LIST

Creating a bucket list can give you some insight into what is important to you, and what you really want to achieve in your life.

Write down a list of things that you want to do before you die.

_____

_____

_____

_____

_____

_____

_____

_____

_____

What steps do you need to take now to accomplish the things listed on your bucket list?

_____

_____

_____

_____

_____

_____

_____

_____

_____

ANGER LOG

Week 1

Rank your anger on scale from one to ten. One being lowest and ten being highest.

1   2   3   4   5   6   7   8   9   10

Please explain your ranking for this week

_____

_____

_____

_____

Week 2

Rank your anger on scale from one to ten. One being lowest and ten being highest.

1   2   3   4   5   6   7   8   9   10

Please explain your ranking for this week

_____

_____

_____

_____

Week 3

Rank your anger on scale from one to ten. One being the lowest and ten being highest.

1   2   3   4   5   6   7   8   9   10

Please explain your ranking for this week

_____

_____

_____

_____

_____

Week 4

Rank your anger on scale from one to ten. One being lowest and ten being highest.

1   2   3   4   5   6   7   8   9   10

Please explain your ranking for this week

_____

_____

_____

_____

Week 5

Rank your anger on scale from one to ten. One being lowest and ten being highest.

1   2   3   4   5   6   7   8   9   10

Please explain your ranking for this week

_____

_____

_____

_____

Week 6

Rank your anger on scale from one to ten. One being lowest and ten being highest.

1   2   3   4   5   6   7   8   9   10

Please explain your ranking for this week

_____

_____

_____

Week 7

Rank your anger on scale from one to ten. One being lowest and ten being highest.

1   2   3   4   5   6   7   8   9   10

Please explain your ranking for this week

_____

_____

_____

_____

_____

Week 8

Rank your anger on scale from one to ten. One being lowest and ten being highest.

1   2   3   4   5   6   7   8   9   10

Please explain your ranking for this week

_____

_____

_____

_____

_____

Week 9

Rank your anger on scale from one to ten. One being lowest and ten being highest.

1   2   3   4   5   6   7   8   9   10

Please explain your ranking for this week

_____

_____

_____

_____

_____

Week 10

Rank your anger on scale from one to ten. One being lowest and ten being highest.

1   2   3   4   5   6   7   8   9   10

Please explain your ranking for this week

_____

_____

_____

_____

Week 11

Rank your anger on scale from one to ten. One being lowest and ten being highest.

1   2   3   4   5   6   7   8   9   10

Please explain your ranking for this week

_____

_____

_____

_____

Week 12

Rank your anger on scale from one to ten. One being lowest and ten being highest.

1   2   3   4   5   6   7   8   9   10

Please explain your ranking for this week

_____

_____

_____

_____

RELAPSE PREVENTION

When we are trying to make positive changes in our lives, it is not uncommon to experience one or more relapses. Anybody who has tried to quit smoking or start a new diet knows that falling back into old patterns is all too easy.

While relapses can be frustrating, they can also be valuable learning experiences. Experiencing a relapse can help you to identify what high-risk situations you may need to avoid in the future.

Here are some steps for dealing with a relapse if it happens:

1. Be honest about it—It's easy to feel embarrassed or ashamed when a relapse occurs, but hiding it increases the likelihood of additional relapses in the future. Instead of trying to forget about it or hide it, let a trusted friend or counselor know about your relapse. Holding yourself accountable is crucial.

2. Identify factors that led to the relapse—Did you put yourself into a high-risk situation that you couldn't handle? Did you neglect self-care? Identifying the factors that contributed to the relapse will help you avoid another one from occurring.

3. Make changes to decrease the likelihood of future relapses: The changes that need to be made depend on what led to the relapse, but may include avoiding similar high-risk situations, attending counseling or a support group, or increasing self-care.

4. Get support—Hearing from other people who have been through similar experiences can help you feel less alone. Getting support can also help you avoid feeling too discouraged to try again in the future.

5. Remember that all is not lost—The fact that you had a relapse does not negate all the positive progress that you made. You don't have to start all over; you just need to get back on track!

REFERENCES

Allen, R. (2012), SMART recovery family and friends handbook. Alcohol & Drug Abuse Self-Help Network, Inc.

Cherry, K. (2016). Five components of emotional intelligence. Retrieved from https://www.verywell.com/components-of-emotional-intelligence-2795438

Davis, M, Eshelman, E. R., & McKay, M. (2008). The relaxation & stress reduction workbook, 6th edition. Oakland, CA: New Harbinger Publications, Inc.

Grohol, J. M. (2017). 15 common cognitive distortions. Retrieved from http://psychcentral.com/lib/15-common-cognitive-distortions/

Hayes, S. C. (2005). Get out of your mind & into your life. Oakland, CA: New Harbinger Publications, Inc.

Laurent, S. (2015). Are men angrier than women? Retrieved from https://www.psychologytoday.com/blog/chill-pill/201505/are-men-angrier-women

Martin, B. (2016). Challenging negative self-talk. Retrieved from http://psychcentral.com/lib/challenging-negative-self-talk/

McKay, M., Wood, J. C., & Brantley, J. (2007). The Dialectical behavior therapy skills workbook. Oakland, CA: New Harbinger Publications.

Morin, A. (2015). Seven scientifically proven benefits of gratitude. Retrieved from https://www.psychologytoday.com/blog/what-mentally-strong-people-dont-do/201504/7-scientifi cally-proven-benefits-gratitude

Pratt, K. (2014). Psychology tools: A-B-C-D model for anger management. Retrieved from https://healthypsych.com/psychology-tools-a-b-c-d-model-for-anger-management/

Prisgrove, P. (n.d.). A relapse prevention approach to reducing aggressive behaviour. Retrieved from http://www.aic.gov.au/media_library/publications/proceedings/19/prisgrove.pdf

Ray, L. (2013). Box breathing technique. Retrieved from http://www.livestrong.com/article/74944-box-breathing-technique/

Segal, J., & Smith, M. (2016). Conflict resolution skills. Retrieved from https://www.helpguide.org/articles/relationships/conflict-resolution-skills.htm

Seltzer, L. F. (2008). What your anger may be hiding. Retrieved from https://www.psychologytoday.com/blog/evolution-the-self/200807/what-your-anger-may-be-hidi ng